GRIEVING, HOPE AND SOLACE

When a Loved One Dies in Christ

Albert N. Martin
Cruciform Press | Released August, 2011

To the members and friends of Trinity Baptist
Church who, as my "forever family," wept with
me during my long night of weeping, and who have
rejoiced with me in my extended morning of joy.
– Albert N. Martin

CruciformPress

"This tender book by a much-loved pastor, written after the death of his beloved wife, offers comfort to those in tears. Even our grieving should be disciplined by Scripture and governed by the motive to glorify God. Here we have a rare guidebook to teach us how to grieve with godliness. It is relevant to us all — if not for today, then no doubt for tomorrow."

> **Maurice Roberts**, Minister of Greyfriars Congregation, Inverness, Scotland; author of numerous books, former editor of *Banner of Truth* magazine

"For more than 50 years, Albert N. Martin has preached the Word of God with power. Now he does it in print. Nowhere in life is the truth of the gospel more real than when a loved one dies in Christ. That time, above all other times, is when the believer needs to experience the consolation of Christ in the gospel. In this tender, biblical, experiential, and even evangelistic book, Albert Martin brings his readers into a wonderful encounter with the Lord Jesus. He uses Scripture, pastoral wisdom, and the experience of his dear wife's death to show believers how God sustains his grieving saints. This is a theologically solid and practically valuable little book."

> **Pastor Brian Borgman**, Grace Community Church, Minden, NV, author of *Feelings and Faith* (Crossway)

"I am thankful that Cruciform Press has undertaken the project of printing materials that flow from the wealth of experience that Dr. Albert N. Martin acquired from his nearly half a century of faithful and richly God-blessed pastoral ministry in one congregation in New Jersey. It is rare, indeed, to receive the benefit of that kind of ministerial understanding and wisdom.

"In this book, Dr. Martin combines an understanding of the best of theology and biblical exegesis with all the pathos that a deeply sensitive redeemed man has as he experiences the death of a much-loved spouse. Channel that through the mind and heart of a pastor who senses his divine commission to minister to others what the Lord has taught him in the crucible of painful human experience, and you will have the essence of this precious volume. For pastors and others who counsel, and for those who are going through bereavement themselves, here is balm of Gilead that has its source in the all-wise Father, the Wonderful Counselor, Jesus Christ, and the unique Comforter, the Holy Spirit. Read it to learn, to weep, and to rejoice in the great victory of the death-Conquering Savior!"

Rev. William Shishko, pastor, Orthodox Presbyterian Church, Franklin Square, NY

"Pastor Martin's instruction will enable you to grieve with overcoming faith, to experience the comfort of our triumphant Savior, and to turn the doctrines of the gospel into the victory of resurrection life, hope, and joy. Thank you, Pastor Martin, for instructing us how to grieve well in the Lord."

Alan Dunn, Pastor, Grace Covenant Baptist Church, Flemington, NJ

"Combining simple exposition of important biblical passages with practical application and personal anecdotes, Pastor Martin has with the Lord's help compounded a genuine balm for the wounded spirits of fellow sufferers. Here you will not find pious platitudes but solid evangelical truth delivered in an intensely personal manner. I recommend it heartily with prayers that the God of all comfort will augment the hope of his saints and introduce others to the risen Lord and Savior who alone is able to comfort them, too."

D. Scott Meadows, Pastor, Calvary Baptist , Exeter, NH

"Pastor Martin reminds us that the death of a loved one is not just the end of an earthly course but also a beginning, both for the departed loved one and for ourselves. This is a book full of encouragement and sound counsel. In reading it and meditating on its contents, you will be greatly blessed."

Dr. Robert P. Martin, Emmanuel Reformed Baptist Church, Seattle, WA

Table of Contents

CruciformPress
something new in Christian publishing

Our Books: Short. Clear. Concise. Helpful. Inspiring. Gospel-focused. *Print, ebook, audiobook.*

Monthly Releases: A new book the first day of every month.

Consistent Prices: Every book costs the same.

Subscription Options: Print books or ebooks delivered to you every month, at a discount. Or buy one at a time.

Annual or Monthly Subscriptions
Print Book .... $6.49 per month
Ebook .... $3.99 per month

Non-Subscription Sales
1-5 Print Books .... $8.45 each
6-50 Print Books .... $7.45 each
More than 50 Print Books .... $6.45 each

Grieving, Hope, and Solace: When A Loved One Dies in Christ

Print ISBN: 978-1-936760-26-8
ePub ISBN: 978-1-936760-28-2
Mobipocket ISBN: 978-1-936760-27-5

PREFACE

The Rough Door of Death

It was an ominous day in September of 1998. Marilyn, at that time my wife of 42 years, had just been diagnosed with cancer. That diagnosis was followed by six years of scans, radiation, surgery, and multiple regimens of chemotherapy. God was pleased to use these means to add six more years to Marilyn's earthly pilgrimage.

After being in a coma for three days, on September 20, 2004, at 6:20 a.m., just as the sun was rising, Marilyn died. I saw and heard her expel her last breath. Although in many ways she had been taken from me incrementally during her battle with that wretched disease, the reality of the finality of death and the radical separation it effects swept over me. A few moments later, as I picked up her lifeless body, I found myself asking the question—*What precisely has just happened to Marilyn? What has she experienced, and what is she experiencing now?* Immediately I knew that if I would grieve as I ought, I had to be able to answer that question out of the Scriptures with absolute certainty.

I had experienced much grief and shed many tears during those six years as my wife declined from a beautiful, youthful, healthy, and active 73-year-old woman to a bed-ridden invalid in a coma. Yet, when she actually died, I instinctively knew that I was now confronting grief of a new kind and of a greatly increased measure. With that realization there was born in my heart a passion that, just as I was being called upon to enter a new dimension of Christian experience, I would, by the grace of God, glorify him in that new experience. I felt very keenly the pressure of 1 Corinthians 10:31, "So, whether you eat or drink, or *whatever you do* [including grieving the loss of a godly wife], do all to the glory of God." This is a command, a positive injunction. There is also a negative directive concerning grieving found in 1 Thessalonians 4:13, a directive given to the people of God that we "may *not grieve* as others do who have no hope."

I have been a pastor and a preacher my entire adult life, having the inestimable privilege of preaching and teaching God's Word on thousands of occasions. Indeed, the preparation and delivery of sermons has taken up a substantial portion of almost every week of my life for some 50 years. Much of my own spiritual life has been both shaped and worked out through this regular discipline and privilege of prayer, study, and preparation.

I make note of this so the reader will understand when I say that this book was born from sermons—

sermons which were themselves born out of my own experiences in the wake of Marilyn's death. I desperately needed clarity and comfort for my own soul, so I sought it where I knew it would be found, in the infallible words of Holy Scripture and in prayer. I desperately wanted, by God's grace, to study and learn what it means to grieve a lost loved one in Christ to the glory of God, to carry that out in my own life, and to share what I was learning with others.

And so it was that four weeks after Marilyn's death, I stood before the congregation of Trinity Baptist Church in Montville, New Jersey (the sphere of my pastoral labors for 46 years), and began to preach a series of sermons that came to form the basis for the first six chapters of this book (a second series of sermons, which forms Part Three of this book, would come later). I had preached on suffering many times before, as well as on death and grieving and numerous related subjects. But now I was preaching from a new perspective — the perspective of a man who has held his wife's dead body in his arms.

These were the sermons borne out of my grief, my tears, my travails, my prayers, and my concentrated study of God's Word during the previous four weeks. During that time, I sought to digest as much as can be found in God's Word regarding the questions that had emerged so alive in my heart at the moment Marilyn died: *What precisely had happened to her, where was she now, and what was she experiencing?*

Those sermons were placed on the Internet, and on the basis of very encouraging feedback, it appears God has used them to strengthen and help a number of his people. In the last few years since Marilyn's homegoing, as I have had opportunity to minister in many different settings, I have become increasingly convinced that God's dear people often have fuzzy, imprecise, or even erroneous views of exactly what happens to those who die in Christ. These deficient views rob them of the ability to grieve the death of a loved one to the glory of God. These views also leave them vulnerable to doubts and fears as they contemplate their own inevitable death, should the Lord Jesus delay his coming. It is for the benefit of such, and for the confirmation of the well-instructed, that I offer this book.

As I have indicated, the following pages contain the fruit of my honest effort to collate and explain those biblical passages, precepts, and promises that will enable us to grieve to the glory of God and to the benefit of ourselves and others. However, it would be unbiblical and pastorally irresponsible of me to give the impression that all godly grieving is of the same shape and color. Our natural God-given temperament, as well as the circumstances associated with the death of our loved one, will strongly influence how godly grief expresses itself. As the light of Scripture concerning the essential elements of godly grieving passes through the prism of our own God-constructed individuality, our grief will find expression across a spectrum of colors that will often differ from one grieving soul to another.

No one person's expression of godly grief ought to be seen as *the* biblical paradigm. The Scripture instructs us, "You were bought with a price; do not become slaves of men" (1 Corinthians 7:23). If you are reading this book in association with your own grieving process, be very careful how you seek to implement well-intentioned and even possibly helpful counsel. Never allow anything but clear scriptural directors to guide your conscience.

The apostle John was given a command to write these words: "Blessed are the dead who die in the Lord from now on" (Revelation 14:13). It is my prayer that God will use these pages to help the people of God to understand those things that make death the doorway into indescribable blessedness for everyone who dies in union with Christ. May the Spirit of God also use these pages in those who are not yet "in Christ." If you, my dear reader, are such a one, may you be made jealous for the blessedness that can be yours when you die, if you will turn from your sin and flee to Jesus Christ as your only hope of life and salvation.

Albert N. Martin
Jenison, Michigan
2011

Part One
FOUNDATIONS

One

FOUNDATIONAL PERSPECTIVES

If we will grieve as we ought when death shatters a cherished relationship, we must have a well-grounded and biblically informed understanding of two foundational issues. One issue involves the nature of human beings, and the other the nature of death.

The Dual Nature of Man

According to the Scriptures, human beings are uniquely created "in the image of God" (Genesis 1:26-27). As such, we are created with two distinct components or entities: bodies, and spirits or souls. Our bodies consist in that part of us that is physical, corporeal, touchable, and visible. Yet we have a second entity that the Bible identifies as our spirits or our souls (for our purposes I will consider these two terms effectively interchangeable). Our souls are that part of us that is non-material, invisible, and truly spiritual.

While the Bible everywhere assumes that human

beings comprise both bodies and souls, some texts of Scripture would amount to undiluted nonsense if this were not so. For example, Jesus said, "And do not fear those who kill the *body* but cannot kill the *soul*. Rather fear him who can destroy both *soul* and *body* in hell" (Matthew 10:28). In 1 Thessalonians 5:23 we have the record of Paul's prayer wish for the Thessalonians, in which he states his desire that these believers would be sanctified completely and that their "whole spirit and soul and body be kept blameless at the coming of our Lord Jesus Christ." Paul envisions that at the coming of Christ both their material and immaterial entities would be completely sanctified—that is, made perfectly holy in every respect.

The Essence of Physical Death

In the second place, we must have a biblically framed understanding of *the essence of physical death as imposed upon mankind by God.* According to the Scriptures, our physical death is nothing less than the radical separation of the two entities that compose us. In the experience of death, the body and the soul, which have been joined in one person from conception, are tragically and completely separated one from the other. James 2:26 contains an unmistakably clear affirmation of this fact. Using the reality of death in human beings to highlight another reality, James writes that "the *body* apart from the *spirit* is dead." James assumes that anyone having any measure of rationality and any contact with biblical revelation would understand from these words that the essence of death involves the separation of the body and the spirit. Even the death of our Lord Jesus involved this radical separation of soul and body. We read in Luke 23:46 that Jesus called out with a loud voice, saying, "Father, into your hands I commit my spirit!" His human spirit was taken into the presence of the Father, while his lifeless body yet hung upon the cross and was subsequently taken down and buried in the borrowed tomb of Joseph of Arimathea.

Concerning this separation which is the essence of physical death, two things need to be emphasized, especially in our almost totally secularized, mechanistic, and materialistic age:

- Death is *unnatural.*
- The separation of body and spirit, which is the proximate cause of death, is *temporary.*

Death Is Unnatural

First, we must understand that *death is unnatural, the result of sin.* Death is not a natural part of life. It is, rather, a violent and unnatural intrusion into human experience.

In his very helpful book, *The Promise of the Future,* Cornelis Venema has written:

Contrary to many modern myths about death — that death is a "natural" part of life, the cessation of existence, that there is a natural "dignity" in dying well—that the Bible paints its portrait of death with the most stark and sobering of colors. Nowhere in the Bible is death treated as something natural, as something that can easily be domesticated or treated as "a part of life." No encouragement is given us in the Bible to minimize the terror and fearfulness of death, our "last enemy" (1 Corinthians 15:26).[1]

Death in the human race began with the fall into sin. It is the divinely appointed punishment upon mankind's disobedience in Adam. In Genesis 2:17, Adam is forewarned that if he eats of the forbidden tree, he will surely die. Formed from the dust of the earth and made a living soul through the in-breathing of his Creator, Adam became liable to death through his act of blatant disobedience.

One of the more prominent passages in Scripture dealing with the subject of sin and death is Romans 5:12-21. In that passage, sin and death are inseparably linked. Therefore, as we think of the essence of death, that separation of the soul from the body, we must think of it as an unnatural separation of that which constitutes us, in part, as image-bearers of God.

The Separation of Body and Spirit Is Temporary

Second, we must always remember that this separation of the body and the spirit is a *temporary reality and experience.* All of history is moving to that moment when the Lord Jesus Christ, with the entourage of the hosts of heaven, and accompanied with the voice of the Archangel and the trump of God, will return to this earth in glory and in power. At that time, the souls and bodies of all men will be reunited in the general resurrection and face the subsequent Day of Judgment. Jesus stated this emphatically when he said, "for an hour is coming when all who are in the tombs will hear his voice and come out, those who have done good to the resurrection of life, and those who have done evil to the resurrection of judgment" (John 5:28-29).

In order to grieve in a God-glorifying manner, we must first of all be clear on this sequence of truths:

- We are creatures made in the image of God and composed of two entities—a soul and a body.
- Physical death is the radical separation of soul and body.
- This tragic and awful rending asunder of soul and spirit in death is both *an unnatural event* and *a temporary experience.*

Two
FOUNDATIONAL PRINCIPLES

We were not made for death. The experience tears us apart, literally so in the case of our own death, and emotionally when the deceased is a loved one. Yet when God allowed death to enter the world he also made provision for us to manage our grief and indeed, to glorify him in it.

When my wife died, I wrestled with a burning question—*How shall I grieve so as to bring maximum glory to God in the midst of my grief?* —and it became clear to me that there were several foundational biblical principles that I had to internalize afresh by means of renewed spiritual disciplines. These principles focus on our thoughts, emotions, and beliefs. After all, in Christ, I am no longer obligated to earthly thoughts and emotions, nor should I let them rule me: instead, I can be controlled and therefore contented by the truth of God.

Our Thoughts Are Under Our Control

God holds his children responsible for the control of their thoughts at all times. Two texts of Scripture clearly establish this first principle.

<u>Philippians 4:8</u>. "Finally, brothers, whatever is true, whatever is honorable, whatever is just, whatever is pure, whatever is lovely, whatever is commendable, if there is any excellence, if there is anything worthy of praise, *think about these things*." Taking the clear command of this verse seriously, and applying it diligently to our minds, is essential to godly grieving. The verb rendered "think" means to consider, ponder, and force one's mind to dwell upon the things identified in the text. In other words, you and I are responsible for the direction and focus of our thoughts, even in the midst of the crushing grief precipitated by the death of a dearly loved one. This directive is not suddenly suspended with respect to the man or woman who has been thrust into the cauldron of deep grief. To consider it suspended is not only to reduce our capacity to glorify God, it is to deepen the pain and poverty of our own spiritual and emotional condition. This command, like all others, is for our good.

<u>Colossians 3:1-2.</u> "If then you have been raised with Christ, seek the things that are above, where Christ is, seated at the right hand of God. Set your minds on things that are above, not on things that are

on earth." Once again, we see clearly that we are responsible for the things upon which we set our minds. We are responsible to direct and focus our thoughts upon specifically identified objects, even in the midst of grief and sorrow. In this text those objects are "the things that are above, where Christ is."

The idea here is not that if we truly obey these verses, we will no longer suffer the pain of loss. In my best efforts to fix my thoughts on the things above, I still felt the pain of my wife's absence. Rather, *in the midst of our grief*—which can be painful, sorrowful, lengthy, and at times even debilitating—the kind of grieving that brings glory to God nevertheless includes a grace-motivated determination, in obedience to these verses, to direct our thoughts to the things above. This both glorifies God and helps to ease—not eliminate—the pain and sorrow of our grief.

Our Emotions Are Not Paramount

When Adam and Eve were created in the image of God, their emotional constitution, along with all their other faculties and capacities, perfectly reflected that image. Before their fall into sin, all of their emotions were sinless, never moving in any direction that did not fully mirror those of God himself. However, when sin entered the world, the entirety of the human person— including the emotions—was infected with that sin.

As fallen creatures, we all feel things we ought not

to feel, while we feel other things to a degree that we ought not to feel them. Even when we are regenerated and indwelt by the Holy Spirit, our remaining sin influences the totality of our humanity, including our emotions. As new creatures in Christ, we need to have our emotions informed by the light of the Word of God, the pressure of gospel motives, and the dynamics of the indwelling Holy Spirit.

Our emotions need objective truth to guide them, and the subjective power of the Holy Spirit must harness and channel them in a godly way. Our current cultural climate affords little help to think biblically about this, so consider three texts of Scripture that prove this point.

Ezekiel 24:15-18. God taught the people of Israel a vital lesson through the death of Ezekiel's wife, by giving Ezekiel what might seem like a strange command not to mourn her loss: "Son of man, behold, I am about to take the delight of your eyes away from you at a stroke; yet you shall not mourn or weep, nor shall your tears run down. Sigh, but not aloud; make no mourning for the dead" (24:15-17a). Ezekiel responds in an amazing way: "So I spoke to the people in the morning, and at evening my wife died. And on the next morning I did as I was commanded" (24:18). I cite this text not to suggest that we are not to mourn when we lose a dearly loved one. Rather, I cite it to demonstrate that it is possible for our emotions to be brought under the control of the Word of God.

Ezekiel was able to say, "I did as I was commanded" because he did not regard his natural emotions as having ultimate authority over him.

1 Thessalonians 4:13. "But we do not want you to be uninformed, brothers, about those who are asleep, that you may not grieve as others do who have no hope." In light of the death of their loved ones, Paul informs the minds of the Thessalonians so that what they know and believe will regulate and take precedence over their emotions. Paul obviously expects that the Thessalonians will grieve, yet he wants them to grieve in a distinctly Christian manner—one that will be patently different from the way non-Christians grieve. Again, we see that we must not regard our emotions as ultimate. Rather, the objective truth of the Word of God informing the mind regulates the activity of the emotions through the power of the Holy Spirit.

Romans 12:15. "Rejoice with those who rejoice, weep with those who weep." In giving this directive to all God's people, the Holy Spirit does not insert parentheses, saying "Rejoice (if you happen to be in a rejoicing mood)" or "Weep (if you happen to be in a weeping mood)." You may find yourself in a very exuberant mood, but when you come in contact with a brother or sister who is legitimately in a state of mourning, what should you do? You should recognize that your own present personal emotional state does not have ultimate authority over you. Rather, in Spirit-empowered self control, you can and should direct your mind to the concerns that brought your brother or sister into a weeping state, and you "weep" with them. The same is true with respect to the mandate to "Rejoice with those who rejoice."

Without question, if we will grieve to the glory of God, we must understand this second foundational principle from the Scriptures: *Our emotions were not created by God to have ultimate authority over us.* Where we fail in this area, as in any other, our guilt and sin are covered by the sacrifice of Christ on the cross. Yet the difficulty of this command, and our frequent failure in seeking to obey it, does not alter our calling. We must use the power of the indwelling Spirit to make an ongoing, scripturally directed effort to reign in our emotions.

The Intermediate State Is Real, Yet Temporary

That period of time between the death of one who dies in the Lord and the coming of the Lord Jesus Christ in power and glory has been designated the *intermediate state*, but we do not know much about it. The Scriptures have much more to say concerning the final, glorified state of believers than they do the intermediate state. In fact, the Christian's "hope" is always used in reference to the ultimate state of glorification, when our souls will be joined permanently to new, deathless bodies.

Although the intermediate state is never identified

as our hope, it always leads *to* that hope—it always leads necessarily and certainly to the final state. Moreover, there is sufficient biblical information regarding this temporary condition 1) to enable us to face the intermediate state for ourselves with confidence and joy, and 2) to assist us greatly as we grieve over the loss of a loved one. Indeed, it is this information about the intermediate state that largely accounts for our ability to grieve unlike "those who have no hope."

Therefore, the third foundational principle essential to godly grieving is this: *We must know and firmly believe what the Scriptures teach concerning the present place and condition of our loved ones who die in the Lord.*

As I held in my arms the lifeless body of my wife, I asked myself this question: *What has happened to her in the few moments that have passed since she breathed her last?* The clear teaching of the Scriptures regarding that question profoundly influenced both the nature and the intensity of my subsequent grief. Scripture plainly teaches us four things about the present place and condition of our loved ones who die in the Lord, and we will explore them in Part Two of this book: Starting in the next chapter, we will learn something of the riches that constitute the *immediate sequel* for one who dies *in union with Christ.*

Immediate sequel. I use the phrase "immediate sequel" quite intentionally. Each of the four things we will consider in the next section of this book become the experience of the believer the moment his or her spirit is separated from the body. There is not an instant of intervening time between death and the blessed experience of the four realities we will learn about. Inseparable from the death of every believer in Christ is God's desire to have that dear child more tangibly near, and when this body of sin has been done away with, nothing stands in the way of God immediately fulfilling that desire.

In union with Christ. I use this phrase primarily because I feel the pressure of Revelation 14:13 which says, "Blessed are the dead who *die in the Lord*." That little phrase "in the Lord" is a key phrase in the fully developed New Testament teaching regarding salvation. It underscores the fact that when one is brought to true repentance and faith by the mighty operation of the Holy Spirit, the penitent and believing sinner is brought into a vital and living union with Jesus Christ himself. Hence the terms "in Christ," "in him," and "in whom," that we find scattered throughout the New Testament. Someone has counted more than 150 uses of this terminology in the writings of the apostle Paul alone. The predominance of this set of prepositional phrases underscores the truth stated in Ephesians 1:3 that God has "blessed us *in Christ* with every spiritual blessing." This brief phrase is the most succinct and accurate description of what it means to be a real child of God. [2]

To Glorify God

Throughout Marilyn's lengthy battle with cancer, she and I adopted many little rituals in conjunction with her multiple regimens of chemotherapy, her periodic CT scans, and her regular visits to her oncologist. I will rehearse one such ritual that has great significance in terms of how a spiritually healthy believer anticipates the approach of death.

Marilyn and I had hammered out before God some very clear guidelines concerning the point at which we would accept the inevitable (barring a direct miraculous intervention of God) and desist from any further medical treatments.

Marilyn had her CT scans taken at a local hospital on a Monday morning. The following day I would drive to the hospital and pick up both the films and the radiologist's report. I would go out to the parking lot and sit in my car and read that report. Then I would call Marilyn on my cell phone and convey to her what that report revealed.

On one particular Tuesday, in March 2004, the pathology report contained both good and bad news. When I called Marilyn and apprised her of that fact, she asked me to give her both the good news and the bad news. The good news was that the nodules in her lungs had not grown. The bad news was that there were now multiple metastases in her liver. When I read that portion of the report to her over the phone, her reflexive response, couched in words I shall never forget, was this: "Well, dear, I am going home." There was no hand wringing. There was no string of questions concerning God's right to bring her to this place in her life's history. Was there sadness in facing the fact that most likely in a few months she would leave me in the condition of a grieving widower? Of course. Was there sadness at the thought of leaving children, grandchildren, and deep earthly friendships and relationships? Of course. However, the overriding reality possessing the soul of that dear woman was the fact that God was going to use metastatic cancer in her liver as the rough door by which she would enter "home." Marilyn embraced the fact that as surely as it was true for Peter, God had chosen for her "by what kind of death [she] was to glorify God" (John 21:19).

Part Two

THE INTERMEDIATE STATE

Three
WE ARE ENDOWED WITH MORAL PERFECTION

Those who die in Christ retain full consciousness of their existence and are immediately made perfect in total moral likeness to Christ

Why has God led this world through the great arc of redemptive history? What has been his ultimate purpose? The great goal of God in redemptive grace has always been and remains nothing less than to glorify himself through the complete restoration of his moral image in those he has chosen to save. And the pattern for that restoration is none other than our Lord Jesus Christ himself.

In Romans 8:29 Paul writes, "those whom he foreknew he also predestined to be conformed to the image of his Son." Paul then goes on to assert that all whom God foreknew (that is, loved beforehand with a distinguishing and purposeful love) he predestined to conformity to Christ. Each such individual ultimately will be glorified, or fully conformed to the moral likeness of Christ in body and soul. J. I. Packer stated these truths most helpfully:

> Glorification (so called because it is a manifestation of God in our lives [2 Corinthians 3:18]), is the scriptural name for God's completion of what he began when he regenerated us, namely, our moral and spiritual reconstruction so as to be perfectly and permanently conformed to Christ. Glorification is the work of transforming power whereby God finally turns us into *sinless creatures in deathless bodies* (Author's emphasis).[3]

Believers who are alive at the return of the Lord Jesus will receive this complete conformity to Christ in soul and body all at once. In an instant, in the twinkling of an eye, those "predestined" and alive on that day will be transformed into the moral image of Christ, body and soul simultaneously. However, most of God's children will attain this blessed state in two stages. First comes the perfecting of our *spirits* at death, when we enter the intermediate state. Second comes the perfecting of our *bodies* in the resurrection at the second coming of our Lord Jesus Christ, as we enter the final state.

Here, in this life, we stand by the bedside of a departed loved one and think, *What has now happened?*

What has happened to *your* loved ones who have died
in Christ? The Scriptures are not silent. They tell us
that the moment our loved ones breathe their last,
their spirits, in the full consciousness of their existence,
are immediately made perfect in the moral likeness of
Christ.

Counted Just, Counted Perfect

In Hebrews 12, the writer enumerates the manifold
blessings that all believers in Christ share under the
New Covenant. Among those blessings, we will all
one day come into the company of "the spirits of just
men made perfect" (v 23, ASV). How do these human
spirits in heaven attain their state of perfection? While
they were yet joined to their bodies on earth, at the
moment they truly believed in Christ, two things
happened simultaneously:

Justification. They were given a perfect legal
standing in the court of heaven by being justified (de-
clared righteous) *on the basis of* the perfect obedience
and substitutionary death of the Lord Jesus Christ
(Romans 5:19, 8:1).

Definitive sanctification. By virtue of their union
with Christ, they died to the dominion and the reign
of sin, and began to be personally holy as the "slaves
of righteousness" (Romans 6:18, and see the context
of Romans 6 entirely). This redemptive experience is
called by some theologians "definitive sanctification."[4]

When we thus experience God's saving grace in

Christ, the reign and dominion of sin ends radically and God begins an actual reign of righteousness in the heart and life of the one now united to Christ.

As all true Christians know well, however, it soon becomes quite evident that while sin may no longer *reign* in the believer, it clearly still *remains*. The child of God begins a lifetime of seeking to put to death the habits, the attitudes, the dispositions and perspectives, the words and deeds that were the dominant patterns of his life while he was yet under sin's dominion and reigning power, however long or short that period may have been. At the same time, the true believer begins actively to seek to become more and more like Christ in the cultivation of the fruit of the Spirit and the graces of Christlike character (Galatians 5:22-23, 1 John 2:6, 2 Corinthians 3:18). This experience is most frequently described and defined as "progressive sanctification."[5]

A true believer in a healthy spiritual state experiences great grief because sin yet remains, actively and aggressively working in him. But, blessed be God, the moment that wrestling, struggling, repenting, striving, child of God breathes his or her last breath, God will put forth upon that soul that has left the body a concentration of his sanctifying grace and power that will immediately complete the work of conforming that soul to the moral likeness of Christ. From that very moment, and on into the limitless stretch of eternity, the departing soul of a true believer will never again have one sin to confess, one tinge of coldness of heart to be ashamed of, one inordinate lust or unholy desire to fill him or her with shame and remorse. Furthermore, the soul of that departed child of God will be beautified with all the graces of Christlike love, purity, passion for the glory of God, and every other virtue of soul which Christ possesses as the perfect man. In becoming totally conformed to the moral image of Christ, we do not merge into little gods who partake of the divine essence. Rather, we become sinless *human* souls or spirits.

In the hours and days subsequent to Marilyn's death, I focused my mind upon this wonderful fact that she was now within the company of "just men (and women) made perfect." And this reality caused me to review the history of her life.

When Marilyn was two years old, her parents divorced. She was placed in the sole custody of a kind and caring but utterly pagan and irreligious father who was an outspoken agnostic. However, gospel seeds were sown in her mind and heart by one of the housekeepers whom her father hired to look after her while he was at work. At age 19, while Marilyn was in nurse's training, God brought some vibrant young Christian women across her path who lovingly witnessed to her concerning her need of the salvation offered to sinners in Jesus Christ. The Holy Spirit watered those earlier sown seeds of gospel truth and blessed the witness of those other young women to bring Marilyn into vital union with the Lord Jesus. She became a new creature in Christ (2 Corinthians 5:17).

When I met Marilyn, two years after her conversion, she was still living in the flush of her first love of Christ, as was I, having been converted just a few months prior. Nothing mattered much to us except talking and singing about the Lord Jesus, reading the Bible and praying together, and passing out tracts along with other young men and women inflamed with a passionate love for Christ and a burden to bring the gospel to those around us. It was evident that God had indeed taken out Marilyn's heart of stone, given her a heart of flesh, and made Jesus Christ the "pearl of great price" to her. He had implanted within her a passion to be holy and to be like Christ.

I was privileged to track that initial work of grace flowering out into Marilyn's progressive sanctification over the course of 52 years (four years of courtship, followed by 48 years of married life together). It was my great privilege to witness much of God's work in her: the Holy Spirit enabling her to mortify patterns of sinful thoughts, attitudes, words, and actions, and empowering her to more and more to reflect the image of her dear Savior. However, all that God had done in her subsequent to her conversion at age 19 until her home-going at age 73 could be put in a spiritual thimble compared to the ocean of grace poured upon her and into her the moment she breathed her last. In an instant, her spirit was purged of every last vestige of remaining sin, and she was endowed with the moral perfection of Christ himself.

Are the spirits of just men and women "made perfect" capable of growth? Yes! Are they capable of further development and expansion in knowledge, joy, and eventual usefulness in the new heavens and new earth? Yes! Just as a *perfect* Jesus was able to grow and develop from a *perfect* baby into a *perfect* mature man, and as a *perfect* mature man became a *perfect* Savior, so there will be growth and development in perfect, glorified believers. But as to their *moral condition and existence*, the dead in Christ are now spirits made perfect. Their minds, affections, and wills are fully and unreservedly conformed to the highest standard of the law of God in all its breadth and depth and in all of its penetrating demands. They will be no more perfect 1 million years into the new heavens and new earth than they were at the moment they breathed their last and joined the company of "just men made perfect."

In those first days after Marilyn's home-going, in my effort to handle the deep and crushing grief of my loss, I sought to frame into little maxims the various aspects of the biblical principles with which I wrestled. I would repeat these words to myself and they helped me greatly: *Albert, think more of what Marilyn has gained than of what you have lost.* I reminded myself again and again that she had gained that which is the burning desire of every true believer, even her complete and final release from all sin.

If you were to dig down through the various layers of the heart of a true Christian, in the deepest subterra-

nean level you would discover a passionate longing to
be done with sin forever and to be holy like Jesus. As
we grieve the loss of our loved one, will not the nature
and measure of our grief be moderated by knowing
that the departed now and forever possesses in full
the very thing for which he or she so deeply yearned?
Would we really want our loved one back in this realm
where, in the sovereign plan and purpose of God, we
experience only the first fruits of our salvation?

Child of God, do you understand and firmly
believe that this has been and will be the experience
of everyone who dies "in the Lord?" Will you focus
your mind upon this when God wrenches away from
you a loved one joined to Christ? Are you determined
to fill your mind with this reality as you anticipate
your own death, should the Lord Jesus delay his coming during your lifetime?

And may I lovingly and tenderly address you, my
non-Christian reader? You have read what I have thus
far asserted—what the Scriptures tell us concerning
the things that await the child of God the moment he
or she dies. Please understand that at this moment you
have no such hope. Apart from Christ, your death will
be nothing less than your entrance into a bleak and
horrific state of ultimate outer darkness, where there
will be "weeping and wailing and gnashing of teeth."
But this need not be your experience. In the kindness
of God you are yet alive. You have your rational faculties, and the God who has created you and sustains

your life has so ordered your steps that this book rests presently in your hands. Let the Scriptures, let me, let this book urge you to "flee from the wrath to come" by turning away from your sins and entrusting yourself to Jesus Christ who died in the place of sinners, rose from the dead on the third day, and now sits at the right hand of God the Father. He is ready, able, and willing to receive every sinner who comes to him. He has given this wonderful word of promise, saying, "whoever comes to me I will never cast out" (John 6:37). Added to all of these things, you have an infallible promise from the living God: "everyone who calls on the name of the Lord will be saved" (Romans 10:13).

Four
WE ENTER CHRIST'S PRESENCE

Those who die in Christ retain the full consciousness of their existence and are immediately ushered into the very presence of Christ

Two texts of Scripture unequivocally assert the wonderful fact that serves as the subtitle of this chapter. Every Christian who wishes to grieve well and die well ought to memorize these two passages and reflect frequently upon their teaching.

Second Corinthians 5:6-8. Paul declares to the church at Corinth his conviction that while he is "at home in the body" he is at the same time "away from the Lord." He also declares his preference to "be away from the body and at home with the Lord." Paul is absolutely confident that *the moment his spirit leaves his body, he will instantly be in the presence of the Lord.* And this is true for all who believe in the Lord Jesus:

So *we* are always of good courage. *We* know that while *we* are at home in the body *we* are away from the Lord, for *we* walk by faith, not by sight. Yes, *we* are of good courage, and *we* would rather be away from the body and at home with the Lord.

In every reference, Paul uses "we," not "I." Whether his subject is being at home in the body and absent from the Lord, or being absent from the body and at home with the Lord, Paul constantly uses the first-person plural. The wonder of being instantly with Christ after death is not something reserved for saints of Paul's stature. We will all know the same extraordinary joy.

As an encouragement to memorizing this passage, let me share a brief story. How well I remember an incident many years ago when an older and godly "Mother in Israel"[6] in the congregation died.

Her son, whose family she lived with, had adopted three children, each with severe mental and physical handicaps. The oldest was a boy named Dusty. Although Dusty had the intellectual capacity of a 3- or 4-year-old, he and his grandmother were very close, having lived together in the same house essentially all his life. Dusty was in his early teens at the time of his grandmother's death, and he grieved deeply when she passed away.

Shortly after the death of this dear saint, in my effort to comfort Dusty, I encouraged him to memorize portions of this very text. I used the words found in the King James Version for their consistent rhythmic cadence. I said to him, and then we said together over and over again, "absent from the body, present with the Lord—absent from the body, present with the Lord." I can never forget how Dusty would break into a broad smile from that point on whenever we spoke of his dear grandmother. Sometimes, when he would see me at a distance in the church foyer, he would smile and repeat those same words—"absent from the body, present with the Lord." Those words of truth enabled that boy to grieve with great hope and even joy.

Philippians 1:21-23. In this second passage, Paul affirms his confidence that death will be gain for him, but he also discloses his internal spiritual tug of war:

> For to me to live is Christ, and to die is gain. If I am to live in the flesh, that means fruitful labor for me. Yet which I shall choose I cannot tell. I am hard pressed between the two. My desire is to depart and be with Christ, for that is far better.

On the one hand, he longs to be in the immediate presence of his Savior. On the other hand, he recognizes the Philippians' need for his ongoing apostolic and pastoral labors. In the midst of conveying these thoughts he makes a simple and uncomplicated statement: "My desire is to depart and be with Christ, for that is far better."

Paul clearly does not think of death as ushering in some kind of "soul sleep" or "spirit anesthesia" until the day of resurrection. Further, he does not think of death as commencing the ultimate glorified state in which he will have a body that can run, dance, hug the saints, and do the many things which only *embodied* spirits can do. In fact, later in this very letter he makes it abundantly clear that it is only when the Lord Jesus Christ returns that we will be given glorified bodies: "But our citizenship is in heaven, and from it we await a Savior, the Lord Jesus Christ, who will transform our lowly body to be like his glorious body, by the power that enables him even to subject all things to himself" (Philippians 3:20-21).

Paul knows that if he were to die, he would be fully conscious and in the immediate presence of Christ. This is the "gain" he refers to in Philippians 1:21. Paul recognizes that although he has been given unusual experiences of communion and fellowship with Christ in this life, the great gain in his death would come from actually being with Christ.

Remember, this is the man whose conversion involved seeing the risen Christ in a heavenly vision and hearing the very voice of Christ out of heaven (Acts 9:3-7). This is the man who had been caught up into the third heaven and heard things which it was unlawful for him to repeat (2 Corinthians 12:2-4). This is the man who reports that in a serious crisis, the Lord actually stood by him and spoke to him (Acts 23:11).

Yet, in all of this, he was not "at home" in the immediate, never-to-be-suspended, actual presence of the risen and glorified Christ. Apart from the return of Christ in his lifetime, Paul knew that he must experience death in order to gain more of Christ and to experience the "far better" of being in the immediate presence of his Lord and Savior. And so it is with us.

Dear child of God, have you faced the fact that you have both a right and a duty to know what is the immediate sequel to death for your dearest loved ones who die in Christ? On the basis of these two texts of Scripture, you have a right and a duty to believe and confidently to expect that those who die in Christ are, in the full consciousness of their existence, immediately ushered into the very presence of the glorified Lord Jesus Christ. You can know and rejoice through your tears that their death is their gain, and that their gain is nothing less than ravishing face-to-face communion and fellowship with the Savior who has won their trust and captured the supreme affection of their hearts.

The moment that the soul of a person who dies in Christ leaves the body, one of the prayer requests of Jesus is wonderfully, if partly, answered. In John 17:24, we read Jesus' prayer to his Father, expressed in the language of divine will and purpose: "Father, I desire that they also, whom you have given me, may be with me where I am, to see my glory that you have given me." This chapter of John's Gospel contains the record of what has been commonly called our Lord's

"High Priestly Prayer." Jesus offers all the requests recorded prior to verse 24 as petitions and supplications, but in verse 24, he exerts his regal will and makes it evident that he desires—or more literally, wills—that all of his people may eventually know the blessedness of beholding him in his resurrected glory—the glory he received as he returned to the right hand of the Father and therefore to the glory he had with the Father before the world began (see John 17:5).

C. H. Spurgeon has written some most helpful words about this part of Jesus' prayer:

> Death smites the goodliest of our friends; the most generous, the most prayerful, the most holy, the most devoted must die. And why? It is through Jesus' prevailing prayer—"Father, I will that they also, whom Thou hast given Me, be with Me where I am." It is *that* which bears them on eagle's wings to heaven. Every time a believer mounts from *this earth to paradise, it is an answer to Christ's prayer*. A good old divine remarks, "Many times Jesus and His people pull against one another in prayer. You bend your knee in prayer and say 'Father, I will that Thy saints be with me where *I* am;' Christ says 'Father, I will that they also, whom Thou hast given Me, be with me where I am.'" Thus the disciple is at cross-purposes with his Lord. The soul cannot be in both places: the beloved one cannot be with Christ and with you too. Now, which pleader shall win the

day? If you had your choice; if the King should step from his throne, and say, "Here are two supplicants praying in opposition to one another, which shall be answered?" Oh! I am sure, though it were agony, you would start from your feet, and say, "Jesus, not my will, but Thine be done." You would give up your prayer for your loved one's life, if you could realize the thoughts that Christ is praying in the opposite direction — "Father, I will that they also, whom Thou has given Me, be with me where I am." Lord, Thou shalt have them. By faith we will let them go. [7]

Yes, it is the immediate and conscious presence of our glorified Savior that will greet us when the door of death shuts behind us. Should the believer be alert when dying, he has both the right and the privilege to say with dying Stephen, "Lord Jesus, receive my spirit" (Acts 7:59). While we have no biblical grounds to expect that we, like Stephen, shall be given a vision of "the glory of God, and Jesus standing at the right hand of God" (Acts 7:55), we have the certain word of promise that when we are "absent from the body" we shall find ourselves "at home with the Lord" — yes, even with Christ, which is far better.

A Word about Heaven

Several times already in this book I have used the word *heaven*. It is time for a brief clarification of how this word is used in Scripture.

In Acts 1:10-11, *heaven* is used three times to designate a place to which Jesus ascended in his resurrected, bodily existence. This tells us plainly that somewhere, right now, there is a physical place where Christ is seated at the right hand of God (Colossians 3:1, 1 Peter 3:22). In this place, the presence and glory of God are manifested in a special, unique way. In this place, cherubim and seraphim surround the throne of God in rapturous worship (Revelation 5:11, 7:11). This is the place to which the departed spirits of just men made perfect go when they die in order that they may be "with Christ." Just as the condition of believers after death and before the day of resurrection is called the "intermediate state," so this is often designated as the "intermediate heaven."

By contrast, the eternal state will be ushered in with the return of our Lord Jesus Christ in power and glory. The "place" or context of that eternal state will be formed by the joining of the intermediate, physical heaven to an earth that is every bit as tangible and physical as this earth, but completely renovated and curse-purged—an earth wherein dwells nothing but righteousness (2 Peter 3:11-13). With all impenitent and unbelieving sinners forever banished to outer darkness, the glorified saints, with their perfected spirits now inhabiting deathless bodies, will worship and serve in the immediate presence of God and of the Lamb in this new heaven and new earth (Revelation 21:1-5). Like their resurrected bodies, this new heavens and earth will in many ways resemble the current heavens and earth, even while being vastly superior, vastly preferable, and completely untainted by sin or any trace of Adam's fall.

At the second coming of Christ, therefore, those departed saints who were already "with Christ" in the intermediate heaven shall gain resurrected, renewed, glorified bodies. In a similar although not identical fashion, the intermediate heaven will be joined to a renewed and glorified heavens and earth. As you read Scripture and see the word *heaven* as it applies to those who have died in Christ, remember that it always refers to the one place where Jesus dwells forever, on his throne at the right hand of the Father, in the presence of those who have been purchased by his blood.

Five

WE ENTER THE COMPANY OF SAINTS

Those who die in Christ retain full consciousness of their existence and are immediately brought into the company of all the blood-washed saints of Christ

Each of us enters this world as an individual. No matter the circumstances of our birth, we emerge into the light as a single, cohesive being, bounded and unitary in body, mind, and spirit. Birth is a highly individual experience. Yet we emerge *into* a community — a community of like beings, each of whom has entered it every bit as naked as we did. It will be the same when we die. We leave one place as an individual, and we enter another as a member of a community.

All God's Children

The salvation offered to us in Jesus Christ is always appropriated and applied individually. As the saying goes, God has no grandchildren. Each one of us must individually be born of the Spirit of God if we will see and enter the kingdom of God (John 3:3-5). Each of us must individually exercise repentance towards God and faith toward our Lord Jesus Christ. The Scriptures also clearly assert that each of us will stand as individuals before the living God in the final Day of Judgment. Paul states succinctly this truth taught throughout the Word of God: "So then *each* of us will give an account of *himself* to God" (Romans 14:12). The Bible is not at all embarrassed to emphasize these various aspects of patent and dominant individualism. Whether in birth, in death, in saving grace, or in the Day of Judgment, not one of us is lost in the crowd.

Together in the Final State

Yet God's salvation, though appropriated by individuals as individuals, is not an *individualistic* salvation. In planning, procuring, and applying his saving grace in Christ, God has something more wonderful in view. He is committed to something more than providing and imparting a righteous and legal title to heaven for individuals, and working in those individuals by the Holy Spirit in order to make them perfectly fit for heaven. Rather, God has an ultimate purpose to constitute nothing less than a whole new humanity in Christ. This new humanity he identifies as his church, his bride, his body, his temple, his nation, and his royal priesthood. [8]

In Revelation 21:9 the apostle John tells us that an angel spoke to him saying, "Come, I will show you the Bride, the wife of the Lamb." Then, we read in verses 10-11 that this angel carried John away in the Spirit to a great and high mountain and showed him "the holy city Jerusalem coming down out of heaven from God, having the glory of God, its radiance like a most rare jewel"—the Bride of Christ is likened to a glorious city. The image of a perfectly organized and well-ordered city forces us to realize that the ultimate purpose of God in redemptive grace is to bring into being, in the new heavens and new earth, nothing less than a perfected new humanity.

God instructs us regarding this future community of believers, a community entered through death, so that we might be able to grieve well for those who die in Christ. When the apostle Paul wants to assist the Thessalonian believers in their grieving process, he describes an event that emphasizes the "togetherness" of all God's people at Christ's return:

> For the Lord himself will descend from heaven with a cry of command, with the voice of an Archangel, and with the sound of the trumpet of God. And the dead in Christ will rise first. Then we who are alive, who are left, will be *caught up together with them* in the clouds to meet the Lord in the air, and so *we* will always be with the Lord (1 Thessalonians 4:16-17).

Yes, with the Lord, and also with all of his redeemed ones, in a state of perfect "togetherness" as the glorified people of God.

Our Togetherness Here a Foretaste

Must we await the return of our Lord Jesus before we have any experience of this blessed togetherness of the people of God? Decidedly, no. It is God's purpose to give us a foretaste of this blessedness here and now in the life and fellowship of God's people bound together in biblically ordered visible churches.

The paradigm for the life of such churches is beautifully and succinctly set before us in Acts 2:42. We are told in this passage that the 3,000 individuals who were brought to repentance and faith on the day of Pentecost "devoted themselves to the apostles' teaching and fellowship, to the breaking of bread and the prayers." They gathered together to delight in God's Word and share life together, and the love they had for one another both sustained them and drew others to the gospel. It was a picture of how we *ought* to be—how we were made to be.

Are there not times when we share such joy and intimacy or such selfless and self-giving love that we instinctively say, "Surely, this was nothing less than a taste of heaven!" We experience life in the company of men and women who are yet imperfectly sanctified, who yet struggle with the wretched outcroppings of their remaining sin that so often fractures human relationships, even in the church of Christ. What must it be when the soul of a believer leaves his body and joins the company of "just men made perfect?" (Hebrews 12:23, ASV). There, in the company of those who have been completely conformed to the moral image of Christ and endowed with every grace of Christlike moral character, they all perfectly love their neighbors as they love themselves. No words are misunderstood, no motives are questioned, differing capacities and abilities provoke no envy or jealousy but only add praise to God for the richness of God's gifts and graces perceived in one another. As surely as we love our Lord Jesus for all the moral perfection we see in him, what will be the measure of our love for those perfected in his moral likeness?

Together in the Intermediate State

When you read your Old Testament, do you not experience at times a longing to have a time of intimate fellowship with Abraham, Isaac, and Jacob? Do you not at times feel something approaching an ache in your soul to commune with David, Solomon, and the prophets? Don't you long to meet and interact with those noble women such as Sarah, Abigail, Esther, and Ruth? Then, when you read your New Testament, do you not experience similar longings when you encounter those individuals in the Gospel records whose strong faith and deep devotion to Christ are commended by our Lord Jesus? I am thinking of that unnamed widow who gave her all, the Gentile woman who touched the hem of our Lord's garment, and the Mary who anointed our Lord for his burial with her very expensive ointment. When you read the letters of Peter, Paul, and of John, don't you yearn to see and interact with those men and thank them from the bottom of your heart for their writings, or to ask them precisely what they meant when they wrote this or that particular verse?

As you read the biographies of those men and women who have exemplified a passionate love to Christ and zealous service to advance the kingdom of Christ, do you not experience strong desires to see them and to thank them for the impact the record of their lives has made upon your own life? I refer to Augustine, Calvin, Luther, Whitefield, the Wesleys, Spurgeon, Edwards, Bunyan, Owen, Flavel, Brainerd, the Hodges, Lloyd-Jones, John Murray, and a host of other men and women—the record of whose lives of devotion to Christ and to his service convict us and whose legacy of written works challenge us to "lay hold on that for which also I was laid hold on by Christ Jesus" (Philippians 3:12, ASV). When our loved ones who die in Christ breathe their last, they immediately enter the company of all of those whom we have come to know and love at a distance. Just as we will be face-to-face with our Lord Jesus, we will be face-to-face with all of them as well.

I do not know how disembodied spirits recognize

and communicate with one another. It seems to me that Scripture is virtually silent concerning this matter. One of the strongest hints in Scripture is given to us in Revelation 6:9-11. In those verses John tells us that he actually saw the *souls* of martyrs underneath and the altar in heaven. Furthermore, John records the words that he heard them speak. From what they spoke, it is clear that they have a sense of time and of the fact that the Day of Judgment has not yet arrived. In response to their prayer to the "Sovereign Lord," each was "given a white robe, and told to rest a little longer." It would appear from the context that it was the Lord himself who spoke to them.

When the Lord Jesus Christ returns and reunites our glorified spirits with our resurrected and glorified bodies, we know that we will see one another with real physical eyes, communicate with real physical tongues, and embrace one another with real physical arms. Until then, in the intermediate state, we shall nonetheless be in the midst of a glorious assemblage of blood-bought and Spirit-renewed saints, all of whom are captivated and ravished by the sight of the Lamb in the midst of the throne. It is into such company that our dear loved ones enter the moment they are taken from us in death. When they are taken from us, we must fill our minds with fresh reminders of this blessed fact of biblical revelation. Surely, this will profoundly influence the nature of our grief.

Six
WE ENTER THE PROMISED REST

Those who die in Christ retain full consciousness of their existence and are immediately ushered into the promised rest of Christ

In the preface to this book, I referred to Revelation 14:13. This is a most crucial text when considering the immediate sequel to the death of those who die in the Lord. In this text, John informs us that he heard a voice from heaven commanding him to write the words, "Blessed are the dead who die in the Lord from now on." He then states that there was a confirming word from the Holy Spirit, underscoring the fact that those who die in the Lord from henceforth are "Blessed indeed." The Spirit goes on to say that they are blessed for a very specific reason: those who die in Christ are blessed in their death "that they may rest from their labors."

The Spirit does not say that those who die in the Lord are blessed so that they may be made perfectly like Christ in spirit, or so that they may be with Christ in face-to-face communion with him, or so that they may be gathered into the company of all the saints of Christ. As we have already seen, these three things *are* aspects of the blessedness of dying in the Lord. However, in this text, God is telling us about another strand of this blessing: those who die in the Lord enter into a permanent rest, a rest promised by the Lord to his people.

Yoke, Perseverance, Rest

When considering the words of this text, it is almost impossible not to have our minds drawn back to Matthew 11:28-30. In that text those who are heavy laden, laboring under the galling pressure of an accusing conscience and weary from their own frustrating efforts to attain peace by means of personal effort, are lovingly invited, even graciously commanded, to come to the Lord Jesus in order to find *rest* for their souls. They are also lovingly invited and graciously commanded to take upon themselves the yoke of Christ.

To take that yoke is not to exchange one galling and oppressive burden for another. Rather, the yoke of Christ is consistent with the disposition of Christ, who is "gentle and lowly in heart." Therefore, since any true coming to Christ to be rid of our heavy burden does involve cheerfully and trustingly submitting to the yoke of Christ, it is important for us to recognize that under that yoke we will find that "*his commandments* are not burdensome" (1 John 5:3), and that his yoke is "easy, and [his] burden is light" (Matthew 11:30).

The Ground Is Cursed

That said, for the true Christian there is indeed a yoke *and* a burden. The child of God must live out his days in this world—a world from which God has not yet removed the curse that came upon our first father, Adam. Being relieved of the galling burden of unforgiven sin and the oppressive yoke of bondage to sin, does not relieve a Christian from the implications of that curse conveyed in Genesis 3:17-19:

> Cursed is the ground because of you; in pain shall you eat of it all the days of your life; thorns and thistles it shall bring forth for you; and you shall eat the plants of the field. By the sweat of your face you shall eat bread, till you return to the ground, for out of it you were taken; for you are dust, and to dust you shall return.

We wear the yoke of Christ, and while it is an easy yoke, we still plow a cursed field.

The Labor Is Long

Added to this is the labor of the Christian life, which is described as an arduous race (Hebrews 12:1-2), a

life-and-death battle with fleshly lusts and appetites
(1 Corinthians 9:26-27, 1 Peter 2:11), and an agonizing
wrestling match with the sinister powers of darkness
(Ephesians 6:12). Furthermore, because all of the dif-
ficulties and trials we experience in connection with
our decaying "outward" man (2 Corinthians 4:16), "we
groan, being burdened" (2 Corinthians 5:4). Living in
our broken bodies in this broken world is hard labor.

Therefore, we see in Revelation 14:13 that much
of the blessedness of dying in the Lord is simply "that
they may rest from their labors." As one man has
expressed it:

> Here, responsibilities, pain and temptation. Here,
> harassment by the demonic, persecution by the
> world, disappointment in friends. Here, relent-
> less, remorseless pressure, requiring us to live at
> the limits of our resources and at the very edge of
> endurance. But there, rest: "the battle's o'er, the
> victory won." The turmoil is behind us and the
> danger passed. No more of the burden of unfin-
> ished work or the frustration of in-built limitations.
> No sin to mortify. No self to crucify. No pain to
> face. No enemy to fear.

While we live in this age, we can only seek to
understand and grasp by faith the blessedness of this
promised rest, but our loved ones in Christ who have
passed through death fully know it to the utmost of its

blessed reality. Fixing our minds upon that fact cannot help but enable us to discipline the grief of *our* loss as we contemplate *their* gain.

These four things, then, are the realities that our loved ones who die in the Lord experience as the immediate sequel to their passage through the door of death:

- They are fully conformed to the moral image and likeness of Christ.
- They enjoy the unclouded and immediate presence of Christ.
- They are in the company of all the blood-bought people of Christ.
- They have forever entered into the promised rest of Christ.

When God snatches away one of our loved ones, we must, in dependence upon God and the gracious working of his Spirit, fill our minds with these wonderful gospel facts. Surely, as we do, we will glorify God in our grief and will not violate his clear directive that we "sorrow not as those who have no hope."

For years, one of the words of the apostle Paul in 1 Corinthians 3:22-23 was an enigma to me. In that text Paul states that "whether Paul or Apollos or Cephas or the world or life or death or the present or the future—all are yours, and you are Christ's, and Christ is God's." The one word that troubled me in that text was the word "death." I could not see in what sense "death" was mine. Was not "death" designated as "the last enemy"(1 Corinthians 15:26)? But now that I understand from the Scriptures that death itself has been made a servant of God and of Christ in order to usher all of God's precious children into the fourfold blessing that we have now seen, I understand how it can be designated as the *possession* of every true child of God.

It is in the light of these realities that we are given the key to understanding the words of our Lord Jesus who said "Truly, truly, I say to you, if anyone keeps my word, he will never see death" (John 8:51). As the wages of sin, as the unleashed fury of God upon creatures guilty of high treason against God, death has been fully swallowed up in the death of Jesus our Savior. No one in union with Christ will "see death" come to him in this intrinsically horrific garb. Rather, in the words of a beautiful choral anthem that I heard many years ago, God is being praised in this way:

> Thou hast made death glorious and triumphant,
> For through its portals we enter into the presence
> of the living God.

Many years ago, I was privileged to visit a cemetery in Scotland where some martyred Scottish Covenanter Christians were buried. I came across a statement on one of the tombstones that made an indelible impression upon my mind. Speaking of those who had been martyred at the instigation of apostate religious leaders, the inscription said "Prelates' [9] rage did but chase them up to heaven." In the estimation of the brethren who were spared to bury these prelates, the murderous rage of apostate religious leaders could do nothing more than chase loyal believers to heaven. Likewise cancer, heart attacks, Alzheimer's, car accidents, and whatever other means God may choose to effect our physical death—all these things can do to the children of God is to "chase them up to heaven" to enjoy, in the full consciousness of their existence, the blessed reality of complete rest.

Part Three
FOCAL POINTS FOR BIBLICAL GRIEVING

Seven
WHAT JESUS HAS GAINED

Think more about what Jesus has gained than what we have lost

As I stated in the Preface, it was four weeks after Marilyn's death when I began preaching the sermons that eventually formed the first six chapters of this book. Then, several weeks after that sermon series, I sought to articulate to my people how the very things I had preached to them had worked their way into my ongoing grieving process. I asked one question: "As we contemplate the death of a dearly loved one who has died in union with Christ, how shall we direct our thoughts and our emotions so that our grieving does indeed glorify God?" And I answered that question in terms of five simple axioms that expressed my experience as informed by the teaching of Scripture:

- Consider what Jesus has gained rather than what we have lost.

- Consider what our loved ones in Christ have gained rather than what we have lost.
- Consider the hope we share with the loved one taken from us.
- Consider what God intends to do in and through us as a result of this grief.
- Consider what we are gaining precisely because of the loss.

We will explore these axioms, and the teaching which they represent, in the five brief chapters that make up Part Three of this book. This chapter takes the first axiom: If truth will discipline even our grieving (Philippians 4:8), **we must think more frequently of what Jesus has gained by this death than upon what we have lost.** This is because, at the moment the soul of a Christian is separated from his or her body, Jesus Christ our Savior partially fulfills at least three things: the divine purpose for his own sacrifice, the desire of God's heart, and holy joy.

Fulfillment of Divine Purpose

<u>In the death of one united to Christ, Jesus receives a precious, partial fulfillment of his own redemptive purpose and purchase.</u> According to the Scriptures, God the Father chose us in Christ before the foundation of the world "that we should be holy and blameless before him" (Ephesians 1:4). In other words, God set his free, sovereign, electing love upon

us in eternity past to this end, that by virtue of his own redemptive grace and power we should eventually become "holy and without blemish."

The Lord Jesus took upon himself the full responsibility of procuring this salvation for his people by his own obedient life and sacrificial death. As he did this, the Father's purpose became his passionate goal as well. Ephesians 5:27 clearly affirms that the Christ who loved the church and gave himself up for her, did so for one clear purpose: "so that he might present the church to himself in splendor, without spot or wrinkle or any such thing, that she might be holy and without blemish."

Jesus, as the heavenly Bridegroom, has always had a marvelous purpose and vision in connection with his redemptive activity. That purpose and vision is nothing less than seeing his blood-bought Bride cleansed from every last vestige of sin and fully endowed with every Christ-like grace and virtue. When any true child of God dies, part of that purpose is wondrously fulfilled. Remember, as we saw in chapter three, the moment a believer dies he joins the company of "just men made perfect." The moment he breathes his final breath, God purges from his departing spirit every last remnant of sin, thereby giving to the Lord Jesus that for which he poured out his life unto death: another redeemed spirit presented to him "holy and blameless."

The marriage of the whole Bride must await the resurrection of the bodies of believers at the second coming of Christ. Then, and only then, will the heavenly bridegroom enjoy *to the full* his marriage to his completed and perfected bride. However, the Lord Jesus does receive with delight those spirits made perfect as the reward of his suffering on their behalf. Because this is true, you must learn to say yourself, *Yes, I have lost my loved one, but my Lord Jesus Christ has seen fulfilled another precious portion of the reward of his sufferings. In the midst of my grief, shall I not rejoice in his satisfaction?*

His Heart's Desire

<u>In the death of one united to Christ, Jesus gains the desire of his heart expressed in John 17:24.</u> Some of the most wonderful promises in the Word of God concern the fact that Christ is always with us. For example, Jesus said to his disciples "And behold, I am with you always, to the end of the age" (Matthew 28:20). Who can measure the ocean of comfort given to the people of God throughout the centuries from those precious words of Psalm 23:4, "Even though I walk through the valley of the shadow of death, I will fear no evil, for you are with me; your rod and your staff, they comfort me." A host of God's children have savored much sweetness from the wonderful promise of Isaiah 41:10, in which God assures us: "Fear not, for I am with you; be not dismayed, for I am your God."

However, as our Lord is about to leave his disciples by way of his death, resurrection, and ascension back to heaven, he reveals in John 17:24 that it is

his will for his own to be with him where he is. But
if he will have the desire of his heart, we must leave
the place where we are and go where he is. Prior to
his return in power and glory, the only way for that
prayer to be answered is for the believer to die and go
to "be with Christ, which is far better." (Enoch and
Elijah were the only two human beings who bypassed
the door of death in their entrance to heaven).

My heart breaks when I lose a loved one who is
therefore no longer with me. But if that loved one
belonged to Jesus, then death serves as the means for
Jesus to receive the desire of his heart. All the departed
in Christ are now "with him where he is." In the
midst of my grief, shall I not rejoice that his prayer has
seen a further incremental fulfillment?

Added Joy

__In the death of one united to Christ, Jesus receives
a new dimension of joy.__ Concerning our Lord Jesus,
we read in Hebrews 12:2 that "for the joy that was set
before him [he] endured the cross, despising the shame,
and is seated at the right hand of the throne of God."
Precisely what is "the joy that was set before him"?
Ultimately, it must be the joy that will be his when, at
the marriage supper of the Lamb, he finally sees his
heart's desire (see John 17:24) fulfilled: it must be the joy
he will have when he finally sits down to feast with his
perfected and glorified Bride, the church (Revelation
19:6-9).

Luke 15 contains the record of three parables spoken by our Lord to illustrate why he "receives sinners and eats with them." In the parables of the lost sheep, the lost coin, and the lost son, our Lord speaks of a common denominator of joy *in heaven* when that which was lost is now found. While the angels join in heaven's joy, that joy is primarily the joy of God himself as he receives back to himself the previously lost sinner. This joy of God the Father was being mirrored in the very actions of Jesus on earth as he received and dined with sinners.

God rejoices when the sinner leaves the hog pens and is taken out of the place of danger and lostness. What kind and what measure of joy must our Savior have when the returning sinner, having passed through death's door, becomes the perfected saint? At that moment, Jesus sees his own image now perfectly reflected in a spirit "made perfect," with all of its sin purged away and beautified with every Christ-like grace. Who would want to rob this joy from the very one who died for us?

Whatever we lose in the death of dearly loved ones, remember this. We did not leave the privileges, the glories, and the joys of heaven itself in order to save our loved ones from eternal damnation. We did not undergo the agony of Gethsemane with its bloody sweat, nor did we endure the spit-drenched face, the buffeting, the scourge-shredded back, the torturous act of crucifixion, the darkened face of God the Father, or the pain of hell itself, vicariously endured. Jesus has much more claim on our loved ones than we do. Let us dare not entertain secret thoughts—manifestations of unmortified self-will—that God is unfair in taking them from us. Instead, when *our loved one had become our loss,* we must consciously and deliberately direct our thoughts to *the joy that has become Jesus' gain.* Remember this clear and stirring declaration: "Precious in the sight of the Lord is the death of his saints" (Psalm 116:15).

Eight
WHAT OUR LOVED ONE HAS GAINED

Think more about what our loved one has gained than what we have lost

In Part Two of this book, we considered those four wonderful realities that make death "gain" to believers:

- At death, we are endowed with moral perfection.
- At death, we enter Christ's presence.
- At death, we enter the company of saints.
- At death, we enter the promised rest.

When we feel most deeply the pain of our loss, we must call to mind these realities. If we will glorify God as we grieve the loss of a loved one, *we must think more frequently of the things our loved one has gained than of what we have lost.*

For several months after Marilyn's death I would

awake every Lord's Day morning especially conscious of the aching loneliness of being a widower. As I would make my way to the kitchen to prepare my morning coffee, I tried to picture what that day would be for her in the presence of Christ. I pictured her looking down at me with a pitying, yet sinless look and saying, "Oh, Al, you poor creature, still tied to "the body of your humiliation." There you are, trying to wake up thoroughly before you go to your study to worship and pray. I have been worshiping all through the night while you slept, and I'm not a bit tired. I will be worshiping all day today, and I know it will not be a wearisome activity. I will not lack for words to give vent to my felt joy and gratitude, nor will I struggle to find abundant substance for my praise. My spirit has been released from every sinful inhibition and distraction. With abandoned joy I will be engaged in worshiping Christ all day today. And when you go to bed tonight, weary from your labors among God's people, I will still be engaged in worship. No night, no weariness, no need to sleep—nothing now but blessed rest from all the struggles of the life I lived when I was still there with you."

I do not believe our loved ones actually view us here on earth, for I see nothing in Scripture to warrant such an assumption. Rather, I share this bit of fantasy to say that in the midst of our grief, dwelling upon what our loved one has gained will strengthen and encourage us, lightening our load and making it easier for us to exercise personal discipline, so that we may carry out our obligations before God more effectively.

None of our generic Christian responsibilities are negated simply because God has taken away a dearly loved one. We may adjust these duties temporarily when our grief is most intense, but that realistic and temporary adjustment must never drift into actual negation of our God-given duties.

Consider the man who has lost "the wife of his youth" and still has young children in the home. Even in his grief, this man must continue to nurture his children "in the discipline and instruction of the Lord" (Ephesians 6:4). He may not, for example, leave them alone for hours while he mourns in solitude. Such a man must discipline his mind to think more on what his beloved has gained than on what he has lost, so that he can dry his tears and do the work God has yet left him to do. As he meditates on the moral perfection of his wife at rest, enjoying the presence of Jesus among countless saints, he will be able to set his mind and will upon fulfilling his privileges and responsibilities toward his children, who are certainly grieving as well. Imagine the opportunities such a man has in sharing with his children from Scripture the joys that their mother is now experiencing!

Consider also the church life of this same man. He knows that one of his generic Christian duties is to "Rejoice with those who rejoice" and "weep with those who weep" (Romans 12:15). Further, he knows the clear directive of Hebrews 10:25, which calls him to gather with his local church, "not neglecting to meet together, as is the habit of some, but encouraging one another, and all the more as you see the Day drawing near." Rather than allow his grief to be an excuse to mope around the house all weekend, when the next Lord's Day arrives, this man gathers his children and makes his way to the place where God's people assemble for ministry and fellowship. Having tempered his grief with thoughts of all that his beloved has gained in her death, he is emotionally free to seek out those who are weeping or rejoicing, and to enter in to their joy or grief with them.

As we discipline our minds consciously to think of what our loved one has gained, our grief is not canceled. Instead, it is kept from becoming a crippling and distracting grief that can so easily become an imprisoning self-indulgence.

Nine
THE SHARED HOPE OF CHRISTIANS

Consider the hope we share in common with the loved one who has been taken from us

I am confident that Marilyn right now has a perfected spirit totally conformed to the moral image of Christ, that she is enjoying the immediate presence of Christ, that she is enraptured with the company of the people of Christ, and that she basks in the wonder of the promised rest of Christ. I am confident of this because Scripture plainly teaches these realities for those who die in Christ.

Marilyn's body, however, lies in a plot of earth in a cemetery behind a church building in Pompton Plains, New Jersey. In the weeks following her death, I would visit that plot of ground each Lord's Day after the morning service. There I would shed some tears and give thanks to God for her devoted love and service to me, my children, and above all, to her Lord and his people. Almost every time I stood on that plot of ground, I focused my mind upon something Marilyn and I share presently, even though she is in heaven and I am yet upon the earth. I focused on our biblical hope in the ultimate reunion of our perfected spirits and glorified, resurrected bodies.

That is, in my grief, I sought to *think more frequently of the hope we share in common.*

Our Ultimate Hope

When the Bible speaks of hope for the Christian, it does not speak of a wish or even a strong desire. Biblical hope is *a confident expectation of and longing for a purchased, promised, but not- yet-realized blessing of God's redemptive grace.* And the Bible make very clear that the primary focus of our "hope" is the ultimate completion of our salvation when we receive our resurrected bodies at the return of our Lord Jesus Christ (we touched on this briefly in chapter two). The intermediate state, in spite of all its promised blessedness for the child of God, is nowhere designated as the "hope" of the believer. The believer's hope is the full integration of his glorified body and his perfected soul. It is this that he knows God has promised him, and that Christ has purchased for him. He longs for and looks forward with confident expectation toward the experience of having his perfected soul inhabiting his deathless body. Paul states this general teaching succinctly in Romans 8:23-25:

And not only the creation, but we ourselves who have the firstfruits of the Spirit, groan inwardly as we wait eagerly for our adoption as sons, the redemption of our bodies. For in this hope we were saved. Now hope that is seen is not hope. For who hopes for what he sees? But if we hope for what we do not see, we wait for it with patience.

Sinless souls inhabiting deathless bodies—we share *that* hope. Revelation 6:9-11 indicates that the perfected spirits in heaven know that this hope has not yet fully come, and they long for its arrival. They pray for it there, under the altar of God, suffused with the believer's ultimate hope. This final hope, this matter of being clothed with a sinless, deathless resurrection body, will make all the more exquisite and wonderful the eternal realities already enjoyed by those who are with Christ in the intermediate state.

Just as those in the intermediate state wait in hope for their resurrected bodies, so we here on earth "groan, longing to put on our heavenly dwelling" (2 Corinthians 5:2). Or, in the words of the apostle Paul "we await a Savior, the Lord Jesus Christ, who will transform our lowly body to be like his glorious body, by the power that enables him even to subject all things to himself" (Philippians 3:20-21). Perhaps most wonderful of all, the proto-type of the body that we will receive is nothing less than the glorious, resur-rected, and deathless body of our Lord Jesus Christ.

Up until Marilyn was diagnosed with cancer, we had spoken occasionally about the necessity of obtaining burial plots. Not until we were well into her six-year battle with cancer did we finally obtain those plots, though. And from the very beginning of our taking legal possession of them, Marilyn identified them as our "Resurrection Beds."

In the last months of her earthly sojourn, when it was evident that God was permitting the cancer to take its toll upon her body, she embraced with noble grace and dignity the many indignities connected with the loss of much of her physical beauty and strength. I vividly remember kneeling by her bedside, just a few weeks before she died, and saying to her, "Sweetheart, when God is done with you in the day of resurrection, you will be so beautiful that I will not recognize you. God will have to introduce me to you." Yes, at the Lord's return, she will be raised her from her "Resurrection Bed" in a glorified body! She lived in that hope. She died in that hope. She still throbs with that great, ultimate hope, even in the presence of Christ. As long as I remain here on earth, I will continue to share with her the same hope. And should the Lord Jesus delay his coming in my lifetime, I trust, by the grace of God, to die in that same hope.

My grieving sister, my grieving brother—if you would grieve to the glory of God, then remember that you share a common hope with that one whom God has seen fit to wrench from you in his unfailing love, his inscrutable wisdom, and his unfettered sovereignty. Grieve your loss, yes, but never as those "who have no hope" (1 Thessalonians 4:13). Spurgeon stated it in his own inimitable way when he wrote: "Tears are permitted, but they must glisten in the light of faith and hope."[10]

Ten
GOD'S PURPOSES IN US THROUGH THIS DEATH

Consider what God intends to do in and through us as a result of this grief

When a servant of God prays from the heart, "Lord, do whatever you need to do to me and in me to make me a better shepherd of your people," we have no idea how God will answer. For me, such a prayer was answered in part by God's severe mercy in taking Marilyn from me.

I knew that following Marilyn's death, if the Lord Jesus would both delay his return and preserve my life and health, the next 10 or 15 years would bring me many opportunities to minister to newly grieving widows and widowers from among the precious members of Trinity Baptist Church. As I prayed about this, God enabled me to say from the heart, "Lord, if taking the wife of my youth in this way is your means of enlarging my heart and further equipping me to minister to your grieving saints, then do the necessary work in me, to the end that you may effect a deeper and richer ministry of comfort through me."

I trust that in some measure this book is an answer to those prayers.

Let us now briefly **consider what God intends to do in and through us as a result of our grief.**

Comfort My People

Paul writes in 2 Corinthians 1:3-4, "Blessed be the God and Father of our Lord Jesus Christ, the Father of mercies and God of all comfort, who comforts us in all our affliction, so that we may be able to comfort those who are in any affliction, with the comfort with which we ourselves are comforted by God." God himself is the ultimate source of all the true consolation and comfort of his children. Yet, according to this text, *God often mediates his comfort through human instruments.*

Paul understood this principle clearly. As this understanding was joined to his passionate commitment to live a life of selfless service to others, he was able to say, "If we are afflicted, it is for your comfort and salvation; and if we are comforted, it is for your comfort, which you experience when you patiently endure the same sufferings that we suffer" (2 Corinthians 1:6).

Although the "us" and the "we" in these passages refer to Paul and Timothy, the principle embedded in the text extends beyond those particular individuals. It extends, in fact, to all true children of God. The New

Testament is replete with exhortations and commands to all of God's people to consider themselves responsible and greatly privileged to minister to one another.

Note especially 1 Thessalonians 4:18, where Paul commands all the Thessalonians, and us as well, to "Therefore encourage one another with these words." Here, as we have already noted, he is actually writing to believers grieving over the loss of loved ones who have died in union with Christ. The apostle envisions the various members of the church surrounding grieving brothers or sisters and bringing comfort by speaking words of truth, ministering in such a way as to impart courage and strength so that those grieving will not grieve "as others do who have no hope."

Of course, the best human instruments for mediating God's comfort to others are often those who have experienced his comfort in their own intense affliction. Those who have experienced God's special comfort in this way are particularly well-suited to draw near to grieving brethren and share with them something of the comfort with which God has comforted them (2 Corinthians 1:4).

Thus, as we seek to grieve to the glory of God, we must think of that which God intends to do *through us*, as a result of what he is doing *in us* and *for us* in our grief.

Positioned to Give Comfort

Active membership in a church that emphasizes a truly biblical, expository, Spirit-empowered, earnest, and applicatory ministry of the Word of God offers many long-term benefits, and one is that such a church equips people to minister this necessary comfort one to another. It takes an ongoing diet of sound preaching to equip people in this way. Paul could say of the church at Rome, "I myself am satisfied about you, my brothers, that you yourselves are full of goodness, filled with all knowledge and able to instruct [yes, and comfort] one another" (Romans 15:14). Can this be said of your church?

At the personal level, do you have any holy aspirations to become one who can comfort others by the comfort that you yourself have experienced? Then seek out and give yourself to the life and ministry of a church marked by a truly biblical, expository, Spirit-empowered, earnest, and applicatory ministry of the Word of God. If you are not in such a church, do not allow that fact to hinder you from seeking to give biblical comfort to those who suffer. But do become an active and participating member of a good, sound church as quickly as possible.

Perhaps you are blessedly a member of such a church already. Whatever your circumstances in this regard, as we reach out and receive God's gracious comfort in the midst of our grieving, let us pray along these lines: *My father, you have brought me into this crucible of grief that I may experience more fully the reality of your heart as the God of all comfort. As I am comforted, mold and shape me into a more* *useful instrument to mediate that comfort to others. May I never forget that what you are doing **in me** by your grace is to the end that you may do something new and **through me** as a distributor of that grace to others.*

While engaged in the final stages of writing this book, God was pleased to give me a vivid confirming experience of these realities. A dear sister in Christ, a member for 35 years in the church in New Jersey where I was a pastor, went to be with her Lord after a lengthy battle with kidney cancer. Her husband, one of my closest personal friends, asked me to pay tribute to his wife at her memorial service, and I gladly complied. Two days after the service, he asked me if we could spend some time together.

When we shut the door behind us in a comfortable private setting, this dear brother said, "Well, Pastor, let me tell you why I am here. Now that my wife is gone, I am sailing in uncharted waters. I've not been here before, but you have. Tell me what I need to know and do to honor my Lord as I face the future alone."

For the next hour I attempted to unpack some of the major elements of biblical truth, and their practical application, that God had used to comfort and minister to me in my grief after Marilyn's death. Many of these truths in fact make up the very nuts and bolts of this book. In some respects, that hour with a grieving brother was one of the most precious pastoral ministries I have experienced in the 46 years of my labor in that assembly. When my own heart was crushed with grief at the loss of my wife, I could not have imagined that the eye of God saw and marked out that precious hour years later for me to enjoy the sacred privilege of comforting my friend and brother with the comfort with which God had comforted me.

Eleven
WHAT WE HAVE GAINED

Consider what we are gaining precisely because of this loss

For two weeks after Marilyn died, I enjoyed the companionship of my dear oldest daughter and my godly older sister, herself a widow. They stayed in my home, cooking meals, keeping house, and being "sanctified blotters" for my grief and tears.

One day, when my wife and my sister had returned to their respective responsibilities, I thought, *If ever I needed the support and the strengthening influence of the body of Christ, it is now.* Throughout my ministry I had taught the great truth that the body of Christ must minister to itself in love. I regularly preached and counseled God's people to remember the biblical injunctions to "weep with those who weep" and to "bear one another's burdens." So I went to the phone and called one of the families in the church with whom I had especially strong ties of friendship.

When the wife answered the phone, I asked her a strange question. I said, "Do you know how to put some water in your soup?" Of course, the dear woman wondered what in the world I was asking! I repeated the question and then simply stated that I was inviting myself over to their home for supper in order to give them an opportunity to fulfill those many biblical injunctions concerning the ways in which God's people should minister one to another. One might say adding water to your soup—stretching it to feed a guest—is one way to accomplish that.

Over the next few weeks, a number of church families received my "water in the soup" call. Spending time in the homes of my people thus became a wonderful means of grace, both for them and for me. We would sit about the table sharing incidents from Marilyn's life. When this sharing precipitated my tears, I shed them unashamedly and without apology. Often, their tears mingled with mine, making these precious brothers and sisters mediators to me of the disposition and heart of my sympathetic Savior.

This brings me to the fifth and final axiom that I found helpful in working through my own grief: *We must think of what we gain as a result of the loss of our dearly loved one.*

Yes, we must think of that which Christ has gained, what our departed loved one has gained, the common hope we share with her or him, and the good that God may do to others through our grief. But we

must also give attention to the benefits we ourselves
are gaining through this death.

We Have Opportunity to Grow in Fellowship

As I have just outlined, the greater the tragedy or
sadness, the greater the opportunity for the members of
the body of Christ to minister one to another. Perhaps
we have enjoyed years of ordinary and edifying fellowship within the local body of Christ in which we are
members. Perhaps, in addition to this priceless benefit,
God has given us the added blessing of deep, intimate,
transparent, and time-tested friendships that have
continually enriched us in our pilgrimage. Perhaps we
have read many times Paul's simple statement in 1 Corinthians 12:26 that "If one member suffers, all suffer
together."

But when God plunges us into the turbulent
sea of emotional trauma precipitated by the loss of
a dearly loved one, it is then that the ministry of the
body of Christ and the support of intimate friends can
rise to new levels in our experience. We then can know
as never before how true Paul's words are. In this way,
the death of our loved one has been a benefit to us by
becoming God's means to enhance our appreciation of
his people.

The Word of God Comes More Vividly Alive

As precious as the fellowship of the saints is, who can measure the benefit that comes to us in our deep grief from God's Word? The pressure of that grief suddenly makes many passages of Scripture come vividly to life, when the same verses may not have seemed so dear before then. For many years prior to Marilyn's death, part of my regular devotional exercises involved consecutively reading through the book of Psalms. However, as I read and meditated upon many of those psalms in the context of my grieving, it seemed as though I were reading them for the first time!

We Become More Heavenly Minded

Of course, the tragic loss of a loved one in Christ can serve as a powerful catalyst to make us much more heavenly minded. Just prior to Marilyn's death, one dear brother wrote to me, assuring me of his and his church's prayers for me. In that letter he wrote: "My own heart has ached for you as you spend yourself caring for your flock while you attend most lovingly to the needs of your dear wife. She who will likely precede you into the immeasurable gain of the nearer presence of Christ will remain your helper, as she, by her being there, will serve as a strong cord to draw and keep your affections heavenward."

The man who wrote those words is "no prophet, nor a prophet's son" (Amos 7:14). However, his words are true. After the death of a dearly loved one, we constantly track them up to heaven, as it were, as we attempt to think of their present state and activity. Being drawn upward by our attachment to them does indeed draw us closer to the Savior with whom they now enjoy face-to-face communion.

We Can Live More Intentionally

Finally, as we grieve the loss of a dearly loved one, we gain a greater sense of our own mortality and a renewed determination to live in light of it. When we read Psalm 90, I trust we find ourselves praying with Moses the prayer recorded in verse 12, "So teach us to number our days that we may get a heart of wisdom." But when we have experienced the death of one close to us, we pray that with more earnestness than ever before.

Left to ourselves, we become careless in the duty of numbering our days. We so easily drift into living as though we will be here on this earth forever. No, we do not formally relinquish our conviction that "it is appointed unto men once to die." However, at the practical level we become earthbound. We so quickly lose that sharp edge of urgency manifested in the words of our Lord Jesus, who said, "We must work the works of him who sent me while it is day; night is coming, when no one can work" (John 9:4). Few things more quickly and effectively snap some of the shackles that bind us to this world than does the death of a dearly loved one. Tenderly holding their lifeless form in our arms, or wistfully looking as they lie in a coffin, such experiences become powerful voices. These voices call out, urging us to obtain the wisdom that alone can enable us to live as those who "number our days."

Part Four
ENCOURAGEMENT

Twelve
A WORD TO THE CHRISTIAN READER

There are a number of reasons you may have chosen to read this book. Perhaps you simply wanted to learn what the Bible has to say on such a pressing topic. You may have felt a need to prepare yourself for what appears to be an inevitable experience of upcoming grief. Your desire may have been to become better equipped to counsel and comfort others in their grief, now or in the future. Most directly pertinent of all, you may have been attracted to this book because God has sovereignly brought you into a crucible of deep grief caused by the loss of a dearly loved one.

Whatever the specific motivation behind your reading of this book, the gleanings gathered from a grieving heart have now been spread out before you. Whether you have read these pages out of sheer spiritual curiosity or because you desperately hoped that with God's blessing you might find something to help you regain your emotional and spiritual bearings in the midst of your present trauma of grief, I trust that you found my words to you to be more than pious platitudes, more than self-help pop psychology sprinkled with some Bible verses.

Jesus said, "My sheep hear my voice, and I know them, and they follow me" (John 10:27). I trust you have heard the voice of your heavenly shepherd speaking to you through his own Word within the pages of this book, and that as a result, one of the purposes for which the Scriptures were given to us will be fulfilled in you. That purpose is clearly stated by the apostle Paul in Romans 15:4: "For whatever was written in former days was written for our instruction, that through endurance and through the encouragement of the Scriptures we might have hope."

My dear brother or sister in Christ, I recognize that it may have seemed a bit strange to you at first to be told that you are held responsible by God consciously to direct your thoughts toward him in the midst of your grief. However, I trust that the clear teaching of Philippians 4:8 and Colossians 3:1-3 has persuaded you that this is exactly what you must do. For your good, as well as for his glory, God has graciously commanded you: "Whatever is true . . . lovely . . . worthy of praise, think about these things." In the death of a loved one in Christ we can know and delight in many things that are gloriously true, supremely lovely, and unquestionably worthy of praise.

God commands you to fix your mind upon those very things, even in the midst of your grief.

However, God does not call upon you to do this in your own strength. Later on in the same epistle to the Philippians, Paul records that his ability to experience contentment in diverse circumstances was something he learned to do—not in his own strength, but in the strength of Christ (Philippians 4:13). While the words of Jesus are true, that "apart from me you can do nothing" (John 15:5), it is equally true that if you are united to Christ and indwelt by the Holy Spirit, through Christ you too "can do all things" that he calls you to do.

In bringing this book to a close, I urge you, my fellow believer, to review briefly with me the central issues that I have attempted to establish within these pages from the Word of God. These are the nuts and bolts of the God-given truths calculated to help you to vent your grief in a way that glorifies God—a way that has no affinity with the grief "of those that have no hope."

First of all,

- Make sure that your thinking is thoroughly scriptural concerning the nature of man, created as a body-soul entity, and
- Make sure that your thinking is equally scriptural concerning the nature of death as an unnatural intrusion into the human race as the result of sin.

Then, I lovingly entreat you:

- Meditate long and hard upon those four things which Scripture says constitute the blessedness of dying "in the Lord." In the full consciousness of his or her existence, that loved one:
  1) has been fully conformed to the moral likeness of Christ;
  2) has entered into the immediate presence of Christ;
  3) has joined the illustrious company of all the people of Christ; and
  4) has forever entered in to the promised rest of Christ.

Pray that the Spirit of God will make those truths as real to you as the pain of your present grief.

Finally, go back over those five simple axioms that are the outgrowth of the previously established biblical realities (chapters seven through eleven):

- Think more about what Jesus has gained than what you have lost.
- Think more about what your loved one has gained than what you have lost.
- Consider the hope you share in common with the loved one who has been taken from you.
- Consider what God intends to do in and through you as a result of this grief.

- Consider what you are gaining precisely because of this loss.

Plead with God to give you the grace to bridle your thoughts and to guide them into the paths marked out by these axioms, insofar as you have been persuaded that those axioms are firmly rooted in the Scriptures.

Should God enable you to heed these closing words of counsel and exhortation, it is my prayer that you will have a wonderful sense of peace and joy in the knowledge that by God's grace you are grieving "to the glory of God" and not as those "who have no hope."

Mourning into Dancing

Finally, because I have been sharing with you throughout this book some of the experiences that have informed its content and initiated its preparation, I want to close by giving you a glimpse of some of God's further gracious work on my behalf.

In the weeks before her death, Marilyn, fully aware that she was dying, yet perfectly lucid in mind, spoke clearly to me regarding her desires for me after her death. She couched these desires in three straightforward assertions and directives.

1) Having lived with me for 48 years, Marilyn had come to the settled conviction that God did not

mean for me to be alone, but that in due course I should remarry. On this point, she was emphatic.

2) Should God choose to bring the right woman into my life, I should not be bound by any man-made time frame for remaining a widower.

3) In choosing another wife, I should not simply choose a worthy woman on some objective grounds. Rather, Marilyn's desire for me was that I would "fall madly in love." (It is possible that her choice of words on that point was related to the fact that in her latter weeks she was reading one of the *Mitford Series* novels.)

To make sure I understood her wishes clearly, Marilyn also disclosed these three desires to my dear oldest daughter, who in turn relayed them to me, confirming my understanding.

Some time after Marilyn's death, as the wound of the initial grieving began to heal, I began to feel very keenly the truth of Scripture that, "It is not good that the man should be alone." Because Marilyn had so graciously released me to love again, I began earnestly to cry to God that he might fill the void in my life by bringing me a suitable partner answering to my need.

By a most unusual chain of providential links, God answered those earnest prayers. He brought into my life Dorothy, a godly widow of exceptional Christian character. Not only did Dorothy's proven Christian character and her shared biblical and theological perspectives make her a worthy object of my desires, but also in giving Dorothy to me, God fulfilled Marilyn's wish that I would once more experience the delight of "falling madly in love."

The ESV translation of the Scriptures gives to Psalm 30 the title, "Joy Comes in the Morning." It is a fitting title, for this psalm contains two wonderful statements about the temporary nature of grief and sorrow. David writes, "Weeping may tarry for the night, but joy comes with the morning" (verse 5), and "You have turned for me my mourning into dancing; you have loosed my sackcloth and clothed me with gladness" (verse 11).

Through the clear expression of Marilyn's wishes, and the gracious provision of Dorothy, God has so dealt with me that I have been able to take David's assertions in these two verses and make them my own. With great delight, I close this book by informing you that in March 2006, Dorothy and I were married, and we have known five years of a God-blessed union. Our mourning has indeed been turned into dancing, and our long night of weeping has truly become an extended morning of rejoicing.

Thirteen
A WORD TO THE NON-CHRISTIAN READER

But what of you, my unconverted reader? For some reason, you have persevered in reading this book through to these final pages. Perhaps you have had enough scriptural teaching to know that the devil, who is a liar and a murderer (John 8:44) and the arch-enemy of your soul, has had no part in putting this book into your hands or inclining you to read it thus far. Furthermore, left to the native tendencies of your own evil heart (and in itself, yours is no more evil than mine), you are one who naturally loves darkness and will not come to the light (John 3:19-21). Since these things are true of you, you would never naturally have been disposed to read a book such as this. Can you not discern the goodness of God towards you in the fact that once more, or perhaps for the first time, you have been confronted with the truth of God's Word concerning the great issues of life and death, of heaven and hell?

Since it is the goodness and grace of God that has drawn you to read this book, I would lovingly challenge you not to put it down or thrust it from you simply because you may have been offended by some of the things I just stated. Do not make yourself and your reaction to the truth of God another witness to the fact that "people loved the darkness rather than the light . . . *and [do] not come to the light* lest their [evil] deeds should be exposed" (John 3:19-20). Rather, begin to show yourself as one who truly desires to be among those who "come to the light." I am thankful you have decided to read further.

We All Die

The Bible affirms the evident fact that it is "appointed to man to die once" (Hebrews 9:27a). This is not a matter of faith, but a plain reality that everyone dies. This verse, however, takes us a step further, moving us beyond what we can clearly and simply observe, for Hebrews 9:27 goes on to say that after death comes judgment. According to the words of Jesus recorded in Matthew 25:31-46, in the great Day of Judgment, Jesus Christ himself will sit upon a throne of majestic glory and gather all of the nations before him. He will then separate all men into two categories, and two categories alone—the righteous and the unrighteous. Then, the righteous will be ushered into God's eternal kingdom (verse 34) while the wicked will be cast into "the eternal fire prepared for the devil and his angels" (verse 41). In light of these inescapable future realities that will draw *you* within their scope, nothing is more important for you than to learn whatever you must know and do whatever you must do to be sure that you will receive the gracious welcome of Jesus on that awesome Day.

The Bad News

And what is it that you must know? You must first of all embrace from the heart what we may properly call the "bad news" of Scripture. The Bible clearly teaches that *all mankind* fell into a state of sin, condemnation, and death through the sin of our first father, Adam (Romans 5:12, 18-20). You must embrace the truth that you have within you a powerful bias toward evil and a rebellious disposition toward God. In fact, the Bible clearly asserts that because of your fall into sin through Adam, *and* because of your own personal attitudes and actions, you have no legitimate title to heaven. That is, because of your corrupt nature, you are utterly unfit for heaven, for in that place the standard of goodness and holiness is not other humans, but God himself. The Scriptures unashamedly declare that in your present condition the wrath of God hangs over you and, at the moment of your death, will come crashing down upon you (John 3:36, Romans 1:18).

If you are really serious about learning what you must know about yourself in order to be ready to die, I implore you to take a few minutes to read the following Bible passages. (If you are unfamiliar with the Bible, the

Table of Contents at the front of the Bible can help you find the books mentioned here.) After you read the first passage in Matthew, place a bookmark at the page so that as you read the next passages, you may glance back to Matthew 25 as needed. As you read each passage, think about what God is saying there: read carefully, and plead with God to give you a heart to understand and believe what he says in these passages about you. Read these passages:

1) Matthew 25:31-34
2) John 3:19-20
3) John 3:36
4) Romans 8:7-8
5) Ephesians 2:1-4
6) Jeremiah 17:9
7) Mark 7:21-22
8) Luke 5:31-32

The words you just read accurately describe all human beings in their native state, most certainly myself included. These verses are well worth dwelling on, inasmuch as they represent the true state of our spiritual condition apart from the work of Jesus Christ. Thankfully, however, this bad news is far from the only news the Bible has for us.

The Good News

The same Scriptures that paint such a dark picture of man in his natural, sinful condition also contain the wonderful "good news" — God's gracious provision of an amazing salvation available to those very same sinners. This good news is beautifully summarized in the simple statement of an angel's announcement to Joseph concerning the birth of Jesus. The angel said to Joseph, "you shall call his name Jesus, for he will save his people from their sins" (Matthew 1:21). According to these words and the universal testimony of Holy Scripture, God's saving mercy centers in the person of the incarnate Son of God, the God-man, Christ Jesus. It is he, and he alone, who saves men from sin—that is, from sin's penalty, sin's power, and ultimately even sin's presence.

Further, the Scriptures bear witness to the fact that Jesus is the one who does this saving work. He does not do it primarily by his example, his teaching, or his noble life of loving and self-giving service to mankind. Rather, Jesus saves men and women by having lived a perfect life under the law of God on their behalf (Romans 5:19) and then having died a cruel death on the cross, receiving in that death the outpoured wrath of God upon himself in the place and on behalf of sinful men and women (1 Corinthians 15:1-4, Galatians 3:13). Just before he dismissed his spirit and died, Jesus cried out, "It is finished" (John 19:30). With these words, Jesus was declaring that everything necessary to provide a righteous forgiveness and a just pardon for sinners had been accomplished in his perfect life of obedience and in his substitutionary death for sinners. His bodily resurrection three days later validated his dying cry of an accomplished redemption (Romans 4:25).

Your Decision

The very God who "so loved the world that he gave his only begotten Son" now calls upon you both to *repent* and to *believe* in the Lord Jesus Christ that you might enjoy the blessings of this amazing salvation (Acts 16:31, 20:21).

Repent. Repentance involves your sincere determination to repudiate from the heart your self-willed, self-justifying, and self-worshiping life of settled rebellion against God. When Jesus calls men and women to himself, he does so with these words: "If anyone would come after me, let him *deny himself* and take up his cross and follow me. For whoever would save his life will lose it, but whoever *loses his life* for my sake and the gospel's will save it" (Mark 8:34-35). Paul describes similarly the saving effect of the gospel in all who truly believe: "he died for all, that those who live might no longer *live for themselves* but *for him* who for their sake died and was raised" (2 Corinthians 5:15). And again, in describing the repentance of the Thessalonians, Paul wrote, "you turned to God from idols to serve the living and true God"(1 Thessalonians 1:9).

Believe. And what does it mean truly to "believe on the Lord Jesus Christ"? It means that, forsaking all hope and confidence in anything you *have done* or *have not* done to make yourself right with God, you cast yourself upon Jesus Christ to find salvation—the salvation made possible by his perfect life, his substitutionary death, and his validating resurrection. As someone has beautifully described and defined it, saving faith is "self commitment to him [Christ], in all the glory of his person and perfection of his work, as he is freely and fully offered in the gospel."[11] The wonder and beauty of the gospel is that, in a saving response to that gospel, the Savior and the sinner come into direct contact with one another in the embrace and self-commitment of faith.

No preacher, no priest, no water of baptism, no bread or wafer of the sacrament of the Lord's supper, no penance, no resolutions to do better, no raising of a hand, no walking down an aisle—indeed no religious ritual of any kind must intrude between you, the needy sinner, and the welcoming Savior. The sinner, in the spiritual nakedness of his sinnerhood, must cast himself upon the Savior in all the beauty and power of Christ's saving mercy and grace. Jesus himself has given an amazingly simple promise that you, my friend, *have every right to embrace*. The promise is this: "whoever comes to me I will never cast out" (John 6:37).

Are you living with an underlying dread and terror at the thought of dying? (That is, when you are not managing to block out the thought.) Are you burdened with the oppressive weight of a conscience that accuses you for your many sins and shortcomings? Are you conscious of being bound by the iron chains of sinful passions, appetites, attitudes, and desires? Are you weary with striving to find peace and rest of heart by means of empty religious rituals? If any or all of these things are true of you, then listen again to another wonderful word of promise that issued from the lips of the Lord Jesus Christ, a promise which he speaks to you today with his own living voice as the living Savior and Lord. He says to you, "Come to me, all who labor and are heavy laden, and I will give you rest. Take my yoke upon you, and learn from me, for I am gentle and lowly in heart, and you will find rest for your souls. For my yoke is easy, and my burden is light" (Matthew 11:28-30).

If you will repent and believe on the Lord Jesus Christ, three extraordinary things will occur.

1) All your sins will be forgiven and God will credit you with a perfect righteousness that can never be taken away from you. The Bible calls this state of righteousness "justification" (Acts 13:38-39, Romans 3:24).

2) In the court of heaven you will be legally instated as a son or daughter of the living God, one who will never be disowned or rejected. The Bible calls this blessing "adoption" (Galatians 4:4-6).

3) You will be given the gift of the Holy Spirit, whose indwelling presence will unite you to Jesus Christ, sealing you as God's own special possession and treasure forever (Ephesians 1:13-14, 4:30). From henceforth your identity will be that of a man or woman who is "in Christ" (1 Corinthians 1:30, 2 Corinthians 5:17). Indwelt by the Holy Spirit, and thereby united to Christ, you will be given grace and power to begin to live a life of obedience and

holiness that is well-pleasing to God (Philippians 2:13, John 10:27, 1 John 2:3-4, Romans 6:23).

If you repent and believe on the Lord Jesus Christ, you will be prepared to die safely, and to die well, receiving at the moment of your death those four wonderful blessings identified and described in Part Two of this book. Should God be pleased to use this book to draw you to a saving knowledge of Christ, what a wonderful thing it will be for us eventually to meet and talk with one another in heaven!

Many wonderful things will keep us occupied in the new heavens and on the new earth. Surely one of them will be our reflecting on the surprising ways by which God wove together so many different strands of his providence to bring us to a saving knowledge of himself. In your case, one of those strands will be the fact that God chose to bring me into deep waters of grief upon losing my wife of 48 years. Another strand will be the fact that six years after Marilyn's death, I found myself pressured in my spirit and urged by trusted friends to take the "gleanings" of that grief and record them in this book. A third strand will be how this book came to your hands, and how by the blessing of God it became an instrument to bring you to a saving knowledge of his dear Son.

Just such things will move us to rapturous praise and worship in the age to come, joining the apostle Paul and exclaiming with profound wonder:

Oh, the depth of the riches and wisdom and knowledge of God! How unsearchable are his judgments and how inscrutable his ways! "For who has known the mind of the Lord, or who has been his counselor?" "Or who has given a gift to him that he might be repaid?" For from him and through him and to him are all things. To him be glory forever. Amen. (Romans 11:33-36)

Endnotes

1. Cornelis P. Venema, *The Promise of the Future* (Banner of Truth Trust, 2000), 36-37

2. See "Union With Christ" in John Murray, *Redemption Accomplished and Applied* (Eerdmans, 1955), 161-173

3. J.I. Packer, *Concise Theology* (Tyndale House, 1993), 256, emphasis added.

4. Two chapters on "Definitive Sanctification" in John Murray, *Collected Writings*, Vol. 2 (W & J Mackay Limited, 1977), 277-293

5. Three chapters on "Progressive Sanctification" in Murray, *Collected Writings*, Vol. 2, 294-320

6. A term of honor derived from Judges 5:7.

7. C.H. Spurgeon, *Morning and Evening* (Hendrickson, 1991), 165, emphasis added.

8. See Ephesians 2:19-22, 4:4-16, 5:25-32, and 1 Peter 2:9.

9. A prelate is a high-ranking ecclesiastical officer such as a bishop. These Scottish believers were martyred for their refusal to allow anyone but Christ to dictate their church practices.

10. C.H. Spurgeon, *Beside Still Waters: Words of Comfort for the Soul*, ed. Roy H. Clarke (Thomas Nelson, 1999), 235

11. Murray, *Redemption Accomplished and Applied*, 112